Anxiety

Ricky Emanuel

Series editor: Ivan Ward

ICON BOOKS UK

TOTEM BOOKS USA

Published in the UK in 2000
by Icon Books Ltd., Grange Road,
Duxford, Cambridge CB2 4QF
email: info@iconbooks.co.uk
www.iconbooks.co.uk

Published in the USA in 2001
by Totem Books
Inquiries to: Icon Books Ltd.,
Grange Road, Duxford,
Cambridge CB2 4QF, UK

Distributed in the UK, Europe,
Canada, South Africa and Asia
by the Penguin Group:
Penguin Books Ltd.,
27 Wrights Lane,
London W8 5TZ

In the United States,
distributed to the trade by
National Book Network Inc.,
4720 Boston Way, Lanham,
Maryland 20706

Published in Australia in 2000
by Allen & Unwin Pty. Ltd.,
PO Box 8500, 9 Atchison Street,
St. Leonards, NSW 2065

Library of Congress catalog
card number applied for

Series editor: Ivan Ward

ISBN 1 84046 186 1

Typesetting by Hands Fotoset

Printed and bound in the UK by
Cox & Wyman Ltd., Reading

Introduction

As I begin to write this book I am faced with many anxieties. Will I manage to finish it on time and get it to the publisher? Will it be good enough? Do I know what I want to say and can I say it clearly enough? This seems normal. Facing a new and potentially daunting task gives rise to anxiety in all of us. But how will I cope with these anxieties? Will they overwhelm me and lead to a paralysis of thought and writing, or will they spur me on to 'create' this book? What exactly are these anxieties? And what function, if any, do they have?

If I try to examine exactly what I am anxious about – in other words, think about and name my own emotional experience – then perhaps the anxieties will be mollified. My anxieties are not necessarily irrational ones, although some of them may be. If I examine them more closely, I find that I am anxious about my performance. In other words, will I be judged harshly? Will I be exposed as fraudulent? Do I know enough about the subject to warrant having being asked to write this book? Will I find inspiration from what psychoanalysts call my 'good objects', those mysterious guiding forces within me that are the basis of my security? Will my 'uncertainty cloud' about the whole enterprise be received and held by them, or will I let 'them' down?

This latter anxiety relates to an intimidating or tormenting feeling associated with the fear of being harshly judged, but also a different quality of anxiety, a dejected feeling concerning whether I can be worthy of my good object's expectations of me. This may be recognised by some readers as having something to do with one's conscience, Sigmund Freud's superego and the ego ideal in their relationship to my ego. There are also allusions to the psychoanalyst Melanie Klein's differentiation of the qualities of anxiety divided into persecutory and depressive anxiety, and the problem of containment of this anxiety described by the psychoanalyst Wilfred Bion. We therefore see that the subject of this book is potentially a vast one, covering the whole spectrum of psychoanalysis.

Psychoanalyst Robert Hinshelwood writes: 'The history of psychoanalysis has been one of trying to understand the core anxiety of the human condition.'[1] In this book I will attempt to trace how anxiety has been thought about in psychoanalysis from Freud to the present time, when the world of neuroscience has started to bring fresh insights into psychoanalytic formulations. I hope the examples I use are illustrative of the points I am trying to make, as this is not a theoretical exposition of the development of the concept of anxiety in psychoanalytic thought, but rather an attempt to make everyday life situations faced by all of us more comprehensible from a psycho-analytic point of view.

What is Anxiety?

Anxiety is certainly not just concerned with irrational fear. In many cases it would be irrational *not* to be anxious. For example, a person newly diagnosed as having cancer has every right to be anxious. We would be immediately alarmed if they were not. Although some of that person's fear may be irrational, the fact that he or she is frightened is not.

Irrational anxieties are often found in phobias, like the fear of spiders, thunder, open spaces and so on. Yet sometimes these phobic anxieties have a real basis. A more useful definition, which does not need to invoke real or imagined fears, is 'the response to some as yet unrecognised factor, either in the environment or in the self'. The response may arise from conscious or unconscious sources.[2] This definition captures uncertainty as a central factor in anxiety, and is close to the definition of anxiety coined by Bion as 'a premonition of emotion',[3] which highlights that anxiety is connected to an emotional experience that is likely to be experienced imminently, and emphasises the unknown nature of it.

The notion of premonition also captures something essential about anxiety, as it implies something close to a feeling of dread. Additionally, it firmly places the experience in the body of the person feeling it, as emotions are first and foremost bodily states. We all know what anxiety feels like: butterflies in the stomach, pounding heart, unpleasant sensations or a vague but persistent sense of unease (or dis-ease, as Bion liked to emphasise).

Hinshelwood writes that psychoanalytic theories of anxiety have proliferated over the years and are largely connected with problems arising from different forms of conflict.[4] Freud's thinking about anxiety changed throughout his career, and can be separated into three phases. In the first phase, he believed that anxiety was not directly connected to ideas or thoughts, but was the result of an accumulation of sexual energy or libido produced by abstinence or by unconsummated sexual excitement – for example, *coitus interruptus*. The libido that is unexpressed becomes 'damned up' and, like a toxic substance, is converted into anxiety. Regular sexual practice was felt to release these blockages and liberate anxiety.

An increase in instinctual tension without any possibility of discharge gives rise to experiences of unpleasure, while discharge reducing the build-up of instinctual tension to regain equilibrium or homeostasis can be pleasurable. It is easy to see this in a crowd watching a football match. In football it is often difficult to score a goal, and this uncertainty and build-up of tension creates anxiety. There is an ever increasing anticipation of winning or losing in a stylised conflict situation, where triumph and humiliation are close at hand.

Most spectators in the crowd feel this, resulting in tension, which is easily observed in the faces of the crowd and is felt in a bodily manner by every-one. The shouting of the crowd itself is a socially acceptable method of discharging accumulated energy. Anxiety levels are raised as the supported team fails to score, and especially if the opposing team does. However, when the supported team *does* score, there is a massive release of tension in shouting, jumping and whooping, which is shared by everyone. The sense of pleasurable release is palpable and can seem orgasmic.

The fact that both the unpleasure of the rising tension and the pleasurable release is shared with a large group is helpful in managing the anxiety, as it is dispersed among everyone and thus easier to cope with. There is often an attempt to project the bad feelings into the opposing supporters by, for example, the gloating jeering at the losing team's supporters, when the supported team is winning, as crowds of fingers point at them, signalling the direction of the projection; and the supporters' chant: 'You're not singing, you're not singing anymore!'

It has frequently been said by ardent football supporters that watching your team winning a football match is better than sex. It has been shown that the level of the male sex hormone, testosterone, is raised in supporters when their team has lost at the end of a game. This 'blocked' sexual energy can become toxic in a similar manner to that described by Freud.

If there is no release of the build-up of this toxic tension when, for example, the team loses or the pleasure from the goal scored is removed as the other team equalise, then anxiety can increase and lead to attempts to discharge the tension in inappropriate ways in violent or anti-social behaviour. It is most commonly internalised, giving rise to a feeling akin to a low mood. I am aware that many other complex group and individual factors are at work in this example, and that it is oversimplified for the purposes of clearer exposition.

Repression

At the time when Freud was writing, Victorian sexual repression was rife and many problems encountered in clinical practice arose from the anxiety caused by unacceptable sexual desires. Freud's next theory of anxiety concerned repression. In this phase of his thinking, unacceptable sexual desires, impulses and urges arising from the primitive id come into conflict with 'civilised' societal norms internalised in the person in the form of the ego or superego.

The ego (or self), caught between the demands of its two 'masters', the id and the higher superego (or conscience), represses the ideas connected to the sexual instinctual urges and relegates them to the unconscious. The energy attached to the idea is liberated and can be used for other purposes, which Freud called *sublimation*. The stimulus for the repression is the anxiety in the ego, created by the conflict between the sexual instinct and societal norms.

This is still true today when, for example, a child's desire to 'marry mummy' brings him into supposed conflict with his rival father in external reality or his conscience in internal reality, when he wishes to get rid of his father so that he may have his mother all to himself. This conflict creates anxiety, and the ideas connected with these unacceptable sexual desires towards his mother are repressed and become unconscious. This Oedipal situation will be discussed later (see page 27), as it is the source of many anxieties.

The repressed idea may at times try to force its way back into consciousness – the 'return of the repressed' – and this too can generate anxiety once again in the ego by signalling the emergence of something dangerous.

Automatic and Signal Anxiety

Freud's later thinking about anxiety included a differentiation of two main types of anxiety. The more primitive and primary anxiety relates to a traumatic experience of total disintegration leading to possible annihilation, consequent on being flooded by overwhelming quantities of instinctual tension. Laplanche and Pontalis describe automatic or primary anxiety as:

the subject's reaction each time he finds himself in a traumatic situation – that is, each time he is confronted by an inflow of excitations, whether of external or internal origin, which he is unable to master.[5]

This so-called automatic anxiety is defended against by later signal anxiety, which serves as a warning about the potential emergence of the automatic anxiety – that is, a fear of annihilation.

Freud's later work[6] described '*signal* anxiety, not directly a conflicted instinctual tension but a signal occurring in the ego of an *anticipated* instinctual tension'.[7] Thus the classical psychoanalytic view of anxiety is a signal or warning that something really overwhelmingly awful is just about to happen, so you had better do something about it quickly if you are to survive physically and mentally. It can be likened to a massive electrical storm in the mind.

Freud thought it had connections to the overwhelming experience of birth. The signalling function of anxiety is thus seen as a crucial one, and biologically adapted to warn the organism of danger or a threat to its equilibrium. The anxiety is felt as an increase in bodily or mental tension, and the signals that the organism receives in this way allows it the possibility of taking defensive action towards the perceived danger, which the psycho-analyst Charles Rycroft describes as 'an inwardly directed form of vigilance'.[8]

Both forms of anxiety, signal and automatic, are seen as deriving from the 'infant's mental help-lessness which is a counterpart of its biological helplessness'.[9] The automatic or primary anxiety denotes a spontaneous type of reaction connected to a fear of total dissolution arising from being utterly overwhelmed; it implies no capacity to judge or perceive the origin of the overwhelming stimuli and is thus differentiated from the signal type of anxiety. The function of the signal anxiety is 'to ensure that the primary [*automatic*] anxiety is never experienced by enabling the ego to institute defensive precautions' (my italics).[10] We are thus talking about a situation where we learn to distinguish warning signs or signals learnt from previous bad, unpleasurable or traumatic experiences, to try to avoid them again.

The anxiety thus has a crucial function in preserving the organism from physical or psychic danger. The 'never again' quality is familiar to all of us where we have been hurt or harmed, or overwhelmed. The fear of dissolution of the ego, or disintegrating or ceasing to be, is a primitive anxiety situation for us all. It was thought to have connections to the trauma of birth, but later psychoanalytic thinkers like Melanie Klein and Freud himself in his later works link it to a fear of the death instinct or aggression operating within. Other psychoanalysts like Easter Bick and Bion connect it to a failure of containment, and all these ideas will be discussed later (see pages 49–53).

It is easy to see these fears of disintegration, fragmentation or dissolution in many children's nursery rhymes or stories. Perhaps the best known is 'Humpty Dumpty'. He had a great fall and was in so many pieces that he could not be put back together again by all the King's horses and all the King's men. The anxiety about an irreparable Humpty has many sources. However, for this discussion I am focusing on the fear of dis-integration or automatic anxiety.

One three year old child was so distressed when he heard the first bars of 'Humpty Dumpty' being played on a nursery rhyme cassette (signal anxiety), that he clasped his hands together by his face and pleaded urgently, 'Fast forward Humpty, fast forward Humpty'. If there was no one available to do this, the child would run outside the room and wait until the song was over, at which point he would re-enter. Here we see the operation of signal anxiety in instituting defensive manoeuvres in order to prevent primary anxiety of total disintegration.

It is important to note that Freud's notion of anxiety derives from the fact of life that human infants are helpless creatures and utterly dependent for survival for longer periods of time than any other species on parenting functions to reduce states of internal tension arising from hunger, thirst, danger, cold and so on. This experience of helplessness is seen as the prototype of any situation of trauma. The trauma ensues when the organism cannot regulate its own state and thus becomes overwhelmed. Freud recognised that in any situation of trauma:

What the internal dangers have in common is a loss or separation occasioning a progressive increase in tension until the subject finds himself incapable of mastering the excitations and is overwhelmed by them: this is what defines the state which generates the feeling of helplessness . . . The infant's total helplessness over a relatively long period of time means that the dangers of the external world have a greater importance for it, so that the value of the object which can alone protect it against them and take the place of its former intra-uterine life is enormously enhanced. This biological factor, then, establishes the earliest situations of danger and creates the need to be loved which will accompany the child through the rest of its life.[11]

This fact is crucial in understanding separation anxiety (discussed in more detail on pages 54–61). It is also the foundation for attachment theory developed by John Bowlby, a psychoanalyst and child psychiatrist, which emphasises the primary and biological function of intimate emotional bonds between individuals. The attachment behavioural system is a neurobiological organisation existing within the person, which monitors and appraises situations and events to maintain an internal sense of 'felt security' and safety by seeking proximity or contact with a specific caregiver, termed an attachment figure. Bowlby's use of the term 'anxiety' restricts it to situations of missing someone who is loved and longed for.[12] Child psychotherapist Juliet Hopkins writes:

Anxiety is experienced throughout life when we are

threatened either by a hostile environment, or by
the withdrawal or loss of our attachment figures.[13]

Freud placed the loss of a loved object as one of the most central anxieties. His emphasis on the central role of castration anxiety or the fear of loss of bodily integrity – particularly the penis for the little boy – can also be understood as a variant of separation anxiety or loss. The loss of the penis not only signifies a loss of a source of pleasure; it also has a narcissistic value for the child. It also provides a means, in phantasy and in later sexual life in a symbolised form, of re-establishing the lost primary union with a mother figure.[14]

Emotional regulation through a relationship with a parental or attachment figure is thus crucial for human development. In fact, it has been shown that in situations of continual exposure to trauma in infancy where emotional regulation fails to reduce instinctual tension, the infant remains hyperaroused and hypervigilant to danger, resulting in the failure to develop essential neurological structures necessary for development.[15]

Binding Anxiety

Anxiety therefore has a crucial signalling function for real or imagined dangers in trying to prevent the organism from being overwhelmed by emotion. The idea of anxiety as a 'premonition of emotion' thus implies the possibility that the emotion that may be experienced will be overwhelming and traumatic.

If the emotion can be recognised, it can be bound or attached in some way to an anticipated defensive response or memory or name, and this itself can reduce the anxiety. If you know what something is, at least you can begin to think about it and plan a course of action to try to deal with it. Predictability is a phenomenon that reduces anxiety, since it implies a reduction in uncertainty and helplessness which, as we have seen, are central factors in generating anxiety.

This is easy to observe in the way children love to have previously very frightening stories read to them again and again. One child watching the *Three Little Pigs* cartoon on a Disney video for the first time was terrified by the Big Bad Wolf who could 'eat you up'. The child developed a fear of wolves. Indeed, he would avoid looking at them in books and did not want to listen to the many fairy stories like *Little Red Riding Hood* that featured wolves. He did, however, want to watch the video, which he previously found frightening, again and again. He would anxiously wait for the appearance of the wolf, then start to laugh manically and over loudly as if he had no fear of it at all. He seemed to be forcing himself to confront and master his fear. He used to play a game where he had to be chased, caught and eaten by the wolf, then reverse the situation by chasing and eating the pursuer.

While one could say that the child had developed a phobia about wolves and wanted to avoid situations where he may encounter them, he watched the video over and over again to convince himself he was not helpless and could triumphantly predict the appearance of the wolf. The phobia itself is a way of binding a more generalised anxiety to a specific situation that can then be controlled to some extent. This again reduces the helplessness at the root of the anxiety.

Many phobias are used in this way and are symbols for a deeper anxiety. And, luckily, most are only mildly disabling. Binding anxiety can also be seen in cases of deliberate self-harm, where people cut or inflict pain on themselves. While this can have many causes and meanings, it is often an attempt to localise or locate a non-specific, uncontrolled pain or anxiety to a particular location on the body under the control of the person. An adolescent girl aged sixteen described how, when she saw blood oozing from a cut she made on her arm, not only was inner tension relieved in a blood-letting sort of way, but also the source of the pain could be seen and controlled. It lessened her anxiety, although it had a negative side effect of creating guilt, which is a different type of mental pain.

Melanie Klein's Views of Anxiety

Melanie Klein's work radically altered how anxiety was thought about, as she moved the focus of attention from a generalised anxiety situation favoured by Freud to one of the inner phantasy *content* of the anxiety, to give meaning to it. Klein defined two clearly distinguishable classes of anxiety and defences – namely, the paranoid-schizoid position and the depressive position. She placed the study of anxiety in a central position in psychoanalytic work: 'From the beginning of my psychoanalytic work, my interest was focused on anxiety and its causation.'[16]

Anxiety was also seen to be the main motivation that promotes development, although excessive anxiety can have the opposite effect as well, and lead to an inhibition in development when it is overwhelming and unmanageable.

Klein asserted that infants have an innate quest for knowledge of all kinds, and that the baby's first object of curiosity is the mother's body – what goes on inside it, what it contains, how it relates to her outside appearance and how it is differentiated from the infant's own body. In line with Freud, Klein also felt that there was a continuous interplay within everybody between what may be called life instincts (or love) and the death instinct (or hate), giving rise to ambivalence.

Gratifying experiences with the mother generate

loving impulses, while frustrating experiences generate hatred and rage. It is easy to observe how quickly a baby can flip between these two states and back again. A baby who is waiting to be fed and screaming with rage seems to be in the grip of an intense negative experience. As soon as he (I am using the pronoun 'he' to refer to the baby, with nothing implied by its gender) is picked up and put to the breast, the whole world changes. The baby calms immediately, as if by magic, and is soothed and comforted.

The rising unpleasant instinctual tension within the baby is felt as the presence of a 'bad breast' attacking him, rather than the absence of a 'good breast'. The relieving feed pushes the bad breast away and replaces it with the good breast. In common parlance, people talk of, for example, 'keeping the cold out', implying that they see the cold as a negative intrusive thing, rather than the thermodynamically correct idea of heat escaping or the absence of heat.

The other central tenet in Klein's theory concerns what she termed *unconscious phantasy*. Stated simply, this means that all bodily impulses and emotional experiences have a mental representation in the form of phantasies, which the infant uses to build up his own unique picture of the world. All the time, the baby is trying to make sense of his experience, to construct a model of the world – an internal representation that is continually being modified and tested throughout life. For example, the state of unpleasant instinctual tension arising from hunger can feel like being attacked by a bad object inside. Thus, from the beginning the infant carries within him a dynamic, ever-changing, *alive*, internal world. This world is peopled with representations of the self in relationship to significant others, termed internal objects or parts of the self in relation to each other. The state of these internal objects changes according to what is attributed to them and what is taken in from people outside, our external objects. As psychoanalyst Betty Joseph says:

We know that we build our characters by taking into ourselves – introjecting – our early relation-

ships to our parents and close figures of our infancy and childhood as we experience them, and that we feel about ourselves according to the world we build up inside, our internal world.[17]

The baby's perception of outside reality is dependent on this internalised representation of the world and the relationships within it, and the baby can only make sense of his experience with reference to this. Klein called this the *primacy of psychic reality*. Many of her observations are being confirmed by modern infant research, which has shown that the baby's internal world is much more complicated than we previously imagined and that all perception is mediated by the meaning attached to it by the brain.

The 'world' for the foetus is the inside of the mother's body, and from the infant's point of view it contains everything there is. Klein surmised that the baby was intensely curious about it. She also believed that the baby had unconscious knowledge about intercourse in a rudimentary form, as well as unconscious knowledge of the existence of the father's penis. The mother's body represents in unconscious phantasy 'the treasure house of everything desirable which can only be got from there'.[18]

When the baby is frustrated or angry or in a rage, *in his phantasies* he attacks the mother's body with anything and everything he has at his disposal. It may be through his biting using his powerful jaws and gums, and later teeth, in phantasy to rip, devour, tear, shred, chew up and so on the frustrating breast or nipple. His faeces may be felt to be potentially very dangerous, explosive like bombs that burst from his rectum, or poisonous or contaminating. His urine, experienced as hot or burning, can be used in phantasy to burn up, drown and so on. The mother's body and its contents – particularly the babies inside or the father's penis supposedly incorporated during intercourse – are then felt to be destroyed and damaged, and the infant becomes intensely persecuted by terrors and fears of retaliation for the damage he has caused.

This all sounds most bizarre and far-fetched, but anyone who closely observes children's play or drawings, or who listens to their dreams, will find confirmation of these types of phantasy. Many films contain references to them – particularly horror films. In war atrocities, these phantasies often get acted out.

Klein felt that the most provoking and frightening figure for the infant is when the mother and father are felt to be combined together in a hostile way, which she called the 'bad combined object'. This may occur when the baby feels left out of the parents' bedroom or their private intimate relationship. If the mother is absent from the baby, the baby may assume that she is either with the father or with other children. This is part of the well-known Oedipal situation.

In his phantasy, in the inner world, the infant is felt to attack the parents together, or the mother with some representation of the father inside her, like his penis, resulting in a damaged combined figure which becomes the most frightening and anxiety-provoking object for the baby. These 'bad' internal objects may damage the infant from the inside by the same methods that he had used originally in his attacks, or be felt to be located in bad external objects. His own life is felt to be in danger.

It is quite common for babies to become very frightened of taking the breast, arching their backs, screaming or turning away after they have been angry and frustrated while having to wait during a separation. The absent breast may have been attacked in the baby's mind and thus the baby may fear that the returning breast is hostile to him. The infant is therefore anxious and fearful about retaliatory attacks on him arising from objects inside or outside of him, primarily motivated by the law of the talion – an eye for an eye and a tooth for a tooth – and he uses powerful defences to protect himself and his equilibrium.

This destruction of the mother's body and its parts and contents goes on in the infant's internal world; in external reality the baby can do very little damage except perhaps hurt the mother's nipple or scratch her. It is very reassuring for the baby when his mother returns to him in a friendly manner and the baby sees she has not been destroyed. This confirmation of her survival enables him to gain confidence that there is a distinction between internal and external reality, and that he is not omnipotent – that is, his thought and phantasy are not as magical and powerful as he believes them to be.

Play and Phantasy

I want to give an example of how close observation of the play of a three year old child, Jeff, and his four year old brother, Adam, in a nursery can illuminate the phantasies being expressed in the play. The children depict in their play a series of phantasied attacks on the mother, father and combination of them both. We see the children becoming persecuted following this.

The children were in foster care, having been abandoned by their single mother a few months before the observation took place. Jeff had ferocious tantrums, especially after waking up, when he curled up like a foetus and couldn't bear being looked at.

Jeff is walking around a room in the nursery

dragging his jumper on the floor. His worker asks him to hang it on a peg.

'I can't do it,' Jeff says.

'I'm sure you can,' says his worker – with which, Jeff hangs the jumper on the peg. [*Here we see Jeff feeling he has nothing inside, feeling unable to do anything.*]

The worker is sitting at the pastry table with Jeff's brother Adam. Jeff sits down and says: 'I want to play with you. Can you make me a sausage?'

'You try,' his worker says. 'I'll help you if you can't.'

Jeff rolls a piece of pastry and says to his worker, 'Is this a sausage?'

'Yes,' the worker says. 'That's fine.'

Adam says, 'No, that's a snake.'

Jeff says, 'No, it's not a snake.'

Jeff then rolls the pastry flat with a rolling pin. He puts his rolling pin down and says to his worker, 'How do balls go?'

The worker shows him and says, 'You try and make one.'

Jeff picks up the pastry, rolls it like his worker

showed him and says, 'This is not going to be a sausage.'

Then he says, 'Can you make a necklace for my arm?'

His worker does so and gives it to him. Jeff breaks it into small pieces, throws it on the table and bangs it angrily with the rolling pin. [*The necklace on his arm was something feminine he wanted, perhaps linked to the abandoning mother, and it provokes a smashing, flattening attack with the rolling pin. This flattening of things – potentially good things which turn bad, also like the masculine sausage changing to the snake and ending up flattened – seems connected to his flattened lifeless state in the beginning.*]

Jeff then gets up from the table, sits back down again, gets up again, goes to the corner and picks up a boy doll, saying, 'He has a willy.' [*Refer to the earlier references to sausages, snakes and balls.*]

Jeff puts the doll on the pastry table and Adam sticks pastry over its penis area. Jeff says, 'Willy, willy!', looks at the worker, then sticks pastry on the doll's tummy (the pastry is red) and says,

31

'Bleed *her* belly.' [*Notice the change of sex, and the association to the willy's damaging activity. It implies a bad combination of willy and belly, causing bleeding. Klein called this a phantasy of a bad intercourse. The figure now seems both female and male, a potentially damaged and thus dangerous bad combined object.*]

Adam says, 'We are going to put it on her face' – which he does.

Jeff then puts some pastry in his mouth (which is against the nursery's rules) and says in a challenging way, 'What am I eating?' [*I think he is trying to provoke punishment for his sadistic attacks, as well as identifying with the object of the attack – taking it into him as described above.*]

Adam takes the pastry off the doll's willy. Jeff says, 'Put it back on his willy.' [*That is to make it feminine by covering up the penis, or to represent the idea that the mother and father are fused and combined with each other. It could also represent castration anxiety as described by Freud, with the idea that a woman is like a man with his penis removed.*]

Jeff puts more pastry on the doll's face, saying, 'He doesn't even like me, he can see.' [*Jeff seems to be becoming persecuted by the attacked and damaged object, which may see him and retaliate – think back to his terror on waking up and not wanting to be looked at.*]

Jeff then sits back and watches Adam cover the whole doll with the pastry. Jeff says, 'We're firing her up.' [*That is, burning her up.*]

Adam uses all the pastry and says, 'I want some more.'

The worker says there isn't any more.

Jeff finds a tiny piece and says to Adam, 'Put the pastry on her toes, on *his* toes, sorry.' [*Here especially we see the switch between female and male, probably representing the combination of them both.*]

Jeff shows the worker the small piece of pastry he has in his hand, and says, 'Look, I have pastry; it's pink.'

He gets up and says in a dismissive voice, 'Look at that dolly.'

Then he walks away to the sand.

I think this observation shows vividly how an attack on the mother and her body, including references to the mother and father being combined with each other, leaves her bleeding and fired up, with the man not liking what he is able to see, ripe to retaliate – a very persecutory situation for these little boys. They then turn away and, in a spirit of denial, characteristic of one of the defences of the paranoid-schizoid position, dismiss the whole thing and walk off.

Hinshelwood refers to Klein's use of Freud's term 'Early Anxiety Situation'

. . . to refer to early situations of anxiety or danger for the infant and applied it to her own discovery of the fears arising from the sadistic phantasies of attacking the mother's body and the retaliation expected from it.[19]

Although the early anxiety situation also involves fear of loss of the loved object in a similar manner to that described by Freud, mentioned earlier (see page 18), we are focusing at present on the persecutory anxieties, which involve primarily a threat to the self. The overriding principle is the safety and comfort of the self; poor me. There is little or no concern for the other, and an abdication of personal responsibility.

This persecutory early anxiety situation is responsible for many of the anxieties we all face. For example, if we return to the child frightened of the wolves and the phobia resulting from it (see pages 19–20), it is possible to see that child's fear of the biting wolf who can eat you all up as a fear of retaliation for his own wishes to devour his object, probably the breast in its earliest manifestation, then later his mother and the contents of her body – including his father.

You may remember the reversal game played to gain mastery of this anxiety, when first the child chased his mother and ate her up and then she 'retaliated'. Klein's formulations enable us to make some sense of these primitive yet ubiquitous anxieties and their manifestations in behaviour.

Terror

Terror is a paranoid (highly persecutory) anxiety,

felt in nightmares and anxieties about monsters, ghosts and so on, which leads to a sense of paralysis which 'leaves no avenue of action'.[20]

Meltzer believes that the greatest source of terror arises from the intense fears about dead objects – particularly the mother's babies murdered in psychic reality. Meltzer comments that the 'object of terror cannot even be fled from with success'.[21]

Terror is such a common anxiety that people go to horror films to be terrified to try to gain some control over it, much in the same way as the little boy watched the three little pigs video over and over again. Ghost stories also proliferate in literature. These highly persecutory anxieties surface commonly in bad dreams, and children's play is full of them. The play enables the child to try to express and so bind the anxiety.

A very common anxiety expressed by children (and adults alike!) is the fear of burglars and intruders. This is different from reality-based fears of intruders. Again, Klein's theories can help us make some sense of these fears if we remember that the child in phantasy invades the mother's body – his first house – in order to damage or steal. The resulting retaliatory fears, including robbers coming in the window at night to stab or 'get' the child, are very common. There are many examples of this type of intrusive behaviour that create this type of anxiety – for example, plundering the mother's handbag, or getting between the parents in their bed or when they are being affectionate to each other.

A more vivid example is shown by Peter. In psychotherapy, the child is given the opportunity to express his phantasies in a non-directive way through the medium of play and behaviour.

Peter, aged seven, turns his attention to the window of the psychotherapy room during one of his sessions. He notices that the catch is broken and becomes anxious. His therapist interprets that he is worried that he has broken it. Peter looks at his therapist squarely in the eye as he says this. [*Peter was anxious about damage he may have felt he caused to this portal of entry to the room.*]

Peter decides to become the fixer of the window.

37

His efforts are increasingly complex, Sellotaping the window closed and trying to fix the broken latch. He sets up a complex trap for the intruders, reminding the therapist of the film *Home Alone*, where a child abandoned by his parents triumphs over intruders into the family home with a complex series of traps.

Peter goes over to his toy box , selects a toy tiger, ties it up and wraps it in Sellotape as if imprisoning it. He goes back to the windows and smears glue over the Sellotape, saying, 'If they touch it . . .'

The therapist asks who 'they' are.

'The baddie children who come in,' Peter replies.

'Are they coming to get you?' the therapist asks.

'At night time, when there is thunder, I go to Morris's bed.' [*Morris is his brother.*]

Peter continues, 'They will smash down the door, not the window.'

It is as if he cannot make the room safe enough, that even if the window is secure, they could still come in somewhere else. [*In dreams, often the persecutors cannot be killed; they get up again after being shot and so on, and continue their threat or chase.*]

A little later, Peter goes over to the window and pulls the Sellotape off to release it. [*This seems to signal an attack from the persecutors, although the timing is now under his control so he is not entirely at their helpless mercy.*]

He dives onto the couch in the room and appears to be attacked by the couch cover. He struggles with the cover as if his life depends on it. He thrashes about on the couch, then runs over to his toy box and releases the tiger he had earlier tied up and Sellotaped. At this point he seems to metamorphosise into this tiger. He begins growling and padding around the room on all fours, jumping onto the furniture. He bounds about the room growling, having now become the persecutor rather than the persecuted. [*This identification with the aggressor is a common method for dealing with persecutory anxiety, as it allows the person to project the fear into someone else who becomes the victim of the attack.*]

As Peter pads ominously around the room

growling, snapping and baring his teeth, he suddenly says 'Daddy'.

'Daddy?' his therapist enquires.

'He is drunk,' says Peter, then launches an attack on the pillows of the couch, throwing them about, screaming 'They are babies.'

He grabs the playdough and, throwing it hard against the wall, says it is a baby, too.

'The tiger daddy is having babies. He hates them. He kills them. There are too many babies. They may kill the Daddy.'

As he speaks he throws the playdough around, 'killing it', saying 'I hate babies' in a gruff man's voice clearly identified with the tiger/daddy. The therapist speaks about how frightening this tiger/daddy is, and how Peter tries to become him so as not to be as terrified and helpless as the babies who may be killed must feel.

In this vignette, although we see that Peter is very confused by the source of the anxiety, some clear elements emerge. He is obviously terrified about the intruders getting in, which at first are 'baddie children'. These persecutors quickly become joined with the extremely frightening drunk daddy. His hatred of the rival babies is projected into the daddy, who is now the one who hates babies and wants to kill them.

It is a common defence to project into the father, and especially his penis, the sadism and aggression arising from exclusion from the parental inter-course or 'primal scene' which produces rival babies. People find it strange that young children are interested in their parents' sexuality. They are interested not only because of their own sexual and bodily feelings but also because their parents' sexuality is potentially quite threatening to them.

Peter probably had such murderous wishes towards his parents' intercourse and the threat of other babies produced from it. These babies are attacked ferociously in his phantasy, like the playdough and pillows are in the play. These attacked babies are probably synonymous with the 'baddie children' who are coming to get him. The retaliation is clear, as is his attempt not to feel the primary anxiety of helplessness as discussed earlier. Instead, he identifies with the persecutor and stops being a frightened boy in his bed at night, becoming a fearsome tiger/daddy himself.

Depressive Anxiety

Anxieties about the dangerous condition of the mother's body and, by extension, external reality, interfere with the free exploration of the outside world. These kinds of anxiety based on fears of retaliation and annihilation of the self, termed *persecutory anxieties*, are contrasted with a different kind of anxiety where the prime concern is over the safety or condition of the object – for example, the mother and her body. These are termed *depressive anxieties* by Klein, and relate to the concern and fear of loss of a good object resulting from the child's sadistic attacks on it.

As mentioned earlier (see pages 22–3), intimate relationships are imbued with ambivalence in that both love and hate are felt for the same person. When the baby apprehends the 'selected fact'[22] that the bad and good mother are one and the same person, then the hate and the destructive impulses he feels towards the 'bad' mother are also directed towards the 'good' mother the baby loves; a depressive crisis occurs. The baby becomes concerned about the damage he may have inflicted on the very person he loves most. It is captured in Oscar Wilde's 'Ballad of Reading Gaol': 'Yet each man kills the thing he loves.' It gives rise to a particularly painful kind of anxiety in the baby, and a wish to repair the damage for which he feels responsible. It is, in fact, more painful than persecutory anxiety, as the main focus is guilt, grief, 'What have I done?', remorse, regret and loneliness.

While depressive anxiety involves the fear of loss of love of the person, the quality defined in this anxiety is different from that discussed by Freud. Freud's conception seems more linked to the fear of loss of love leading to the loss of the parents' availability to reduce the instinctual states of the child. This seems to be a more self-centred conception than Klein's idea of depressive anxiety. Since concern for the welfare of the other predominates over concern for the self, characterised by 'poor you' (compared with, in persecutory anxiety, 'poor me'), it also forms the basis for tenderness, empathy and reparative wishes. It involves taking responsibility for one's own feelings and their consequences. Joseph writes:

Of course, toleration of ambivalence with its resultant sense of guilt, if properly elaborated, can and should lessen anxiety, because the awareness of love and concern, and the attempt to do something about this will mitigate anger and resentment and this reduces anxiety.[23]

Thus, the capacity to bear depressive anxiety is a major achievement in the developmental path towards maturity. Many achievements in the world and acts of creativity are thought to be related to the need to make a contribution, to make reparation, arising from tolerating depressive concern, thus demonstrating how anxiety stimulates development. Klein also writes how a baby's anxiety about an object, particularly the persecutory variety, can stimulate the search for new objects which may not be so imbued with persecution, thus enlarging the scope of people and things that the child may relate to in the world.

If either form of anxiety is too great, there can be an inhibition and constriction in the way of relating to the world. Similarly, there can be a marked increase in feelings of guilt, despair and hopelessness if the damage done is believed to be irreparable and thus unforgivable.

Anxieties About Learning

Many learning difficulties can arise from the situation where there is evidence of actual damage to the mother's body. Klein believed that:

It is essential for a favourable development of the desire for knowledge that the mother's body should be felt to be well and unharmed . . . If it is not destroyed, not so much in danger and therefore dangerous itself, the wish to take food for the mind from it can more easily be carried out . . . If the woman's body is felt as a place full of destruction there may be a basic inhibition in the desire for knowledge. Since the inside of the mother's body is the first object of this impulse; in phantasy it is explored and investigated as well as attacked with all the sadistic armoury.[24]

This may sound odd, but think that 'mother nature' is a primary object of knowledge. Specific intellectual inhibitions may result from defences against sadism. These defences may be for persecutory or depressive reasons. So many words and expressions concerned with learning link learning to the feeding and digestive process – for example, 'an appetite for learning', 'take something in', 'food for thought', 'she devoured that book', 'she absorbed it', 'you don't spoon-feed children', 'something was not digested', 'it was just regurgitated', 'swallowed it whole', 'chewed things over' and so on. Psychoanalysts believe that early experiences and situations lay down templates for the personality that recur in different guises throughout development. Anxieties about the feeding process invariably intersect with primitive anxieties and thus can affect the capacity to learn. The phantasy accompanying the particular activity thus determines the outcome of that activity.

In order to be able to read or discover things, you have to be able to look beneath the surface of things, to 'get into' a subject. This implies a kind of penetrating mental activity.

A book is a house for a story.
A rose is a house for a smell.
My head is a house for a secret.
A secret I never will tell.[25]

A word is thus a house for a meaning, and the first house the baby occupies is its mother's body. If the mother's body is felt to be a place 'full of destruction', in Klein's terms, when for example the mother has suffered a stillbirth, miscarriage, abortion or serious illness, then many learning difficulties can stem from this, including reading inhibitions. There may be an anxiety that either she is too fragile to withstand phantasied attacks upon her unborn or born children, or that the child's sadistic phantasies really are as powerful in external reality as they are in internal reality.

It is very common to discover that in the families of children referred with learning difficulties to child and family consultation services, there has often been the death of a baby or child for one reason or another.[26]

As I mentioned earlier (see pages 35–7), the child may respond in a persecutory manner and be terrified and fear retaliation from the dead ghost babies about being alive or occupying their place, or he may react depressively and feel very guilty about what he imagines he has done. He may inhibit his achievements accordingly. Either way, the child's learning is affected.

There are, of course, many other kinds of anxiety that affect the ability to learn, including the operation of envy. A person may inhibit his or her achievements in order not to provoke spoiling and destructive attacks arising from the supposed envy of someone else. Also, there is a need to tolerate the frustration of not knowing something in order to learn something new. In order to discuss this further, since it is a critical point in thinking about growth and change of any sort, it is necessary to discuss the concept of containment of anxiety.

Containment of Anxiety

A central theme of this book is that anxiety, which is a type of mental pain, lies at the heart of all psychoanalytical conceptions. I will use the words 'anxiety' and 'mental pain' interchangeably. A central tenet of the psychoanalytical view is that no development can take place without pain. As we have discussed, too much or too little pain impedes development. Thus the problem of containment and distribution of the mental pain connected with growth and development is our core subject of study. Anxiety is dealt with through the relations with objects, initially the primary attachment figure. The capacity to cope with mental pain in a developmentally enhancing manner depends on the availability from birth, or even pre-natally, of an emotionally receptive or attuned person who can *contain* the infant's primitive communications and help him make sense of his emotional experiences. What does this concept of containment actually mean?

In Bion's theory of container/contained,[27] the development of the capacity to think or be curious in any way, to pay attention or to learn, depends on the baby's experience of being thought about, or having had the experience of somebody being curious or emotionally attentive to him. The baby's psyche is not developed enough to contain powerful feelings of any kind, and is thus absolutely dependent on the availability of some object, usually the mother in the first instance, into whom the baby can rid himself of these feelings. Bion calls this object the *container*, and the raw, unprocessed, undigested emotional material projected into the container, the *contained*.

The baby's crying or other behaviour evokes distress or other feelings in the mother if she is emotionally attentive to her baby. She then has to try to make sense of what the baby is feeling or what his cries mean by reflecting and thinking about what the baby has made her feel, by relating it to her own experience and her experience of the baby, before responding accordingly.

This process, called *reverie* by Bion, is often unconscious. The baby, then, is not only made more comfortable by having his needs met, but is also able to take inside himself the experience of his mother having a space in her mind for him, and he feels understood. As the baby has more and more experiences like this, it enables him to take into his mind a thinking object, a representation of the container/contained experience. He can then use this thinking object, this container, to think for himself about his own experiences. Thus, he begins to develop his own capacity to think about his emotional experiences and have a space in his own mind. A baby thus needs a container to investigate his feelings, to find out what he is feeling and what it means.

What if the mother cannot accept these projections of raw emotion from the baby? What if there is no one to perform the function of containment – that is, bear the unbearable for the baby? The infant's only recourse is to try even harder to evacuate the bad feeling, which is made worse by the experience of feeling misunderstood and not attended to. He does not internalise a container who can think about him or understand him, or help him 'name' his anxieties and differentiate his emotional states based on differential responses to them, but instead takes in a communication-rejecting container.

The infant then cannot make sense of his experience and cannot understand. He seems to experience the container's unwillingness to receive his communications as hostile, and a vicious circle is set up whereby the only choice available to the infant is to try to get rid of his bad experiences with increasing force or, more catastrophically, to give up trying to project his anxieties at all. He does not develop a growth-enhancing method for regulating his emotions, and instead identifies with the characteristics of the faulty container.

Bion describes how in any situation of anxiety there are three ways of dealing with the problem.

The first involves *modulating* the mental pain, 'primarily by thought, leading to understanding and actions that may successfully modify or adapt to the external world, or internalise new qualities into the internal objects that can comfort or strengthen the personality'.[28] Bion talks of the need for us to respect the *facts* of a situation to try to real-ise whatever they are, then act accordingly.

This is to be distinguished from the second method of dealing with pain by trying to *modify* the situation, to try to fit it into how you want it to be. This involves a distortion of the facts by the use of any of the mechanisms of defence – for example, idealise-ing, or denigrate-ing them.

The third more extreme way of dealing with pain is to try to *evade* it altogether, by destroying the capacity to know about reality or ignoring the facts entirely. This leads to ignore-ance, according to Bion. Modulation through thinking, modification through defending, or evasion through obliter-ation are, then, three different ways of coping with anxiety. In order to illustrate these ideas, I want to give an example of one of the most familiar anxieties seen in everyone – separation anxiety.

Separation Anxiety

I mentioned earlier (see pages 49–52) that a baby is absolutely dependent on the existence of a parent to regulate his emotional states. The absence of such a figure, then, gives rise to a particular type of anxiety called separation anxiety.

The separation from a needed and loved figure mobilises attachment behaviour (mentioned on page 17). Separation anxiety can be felt by anyone, of any age, when a loved/needed person is absent, but its roots lie in infancy. How it is dealt with depends on the state of the person's mental apparatus and attachment history. We know that separation is best handled if the child can keep contact with a securely internalised object, or container or working model, that allows him to feel safe in the new environment. I am grateful for Paulo Carignani[29] for allowing me to use these following observations.

Tom, aged twenty-two months, is a child who is finding it excruciating to separate from his mother when she brings him into the nursery. In this observation, soon after he joined the nursery, he runs into the room with his mother and takes out a gun, laughing manically and shooting at everybody. [*From the beginning we see him trying to obliterate his anxiety about coming into this new situation, by being omnipotent and out of touch. All potential dangers are to be got rid of.*]

A teacher says 'Hello' to him, then invites him to come and sit near her and listen to the story she is telling other children. Tom doesn't answer, but instead shoots his gun, making a noise with his mouth. [*We could safely assume that persecutory anxiety prevails, as clearly he is trying to get rid of some baddie threat.*]

Tom subsequently turns towards his mother who is coming into the room, then towards another little boy, who has a little car in his hand. He suddenly grabs this car from the child. The child starts shrieking and tries to get his car back. Tom shouts, then bursts into tears, while the teacher and mother step forward to separate the two children. For a few minutes the teacher tries hopelessly to convince Tom to hand back the car.

When she eventually scolds him in a high voice, Tom yells even more loudly.

The teacher takes the car from Tom and hands it to the other child. Tom throws himself to the floor, crying desperately. The mother looks terribly anxious. She stands near him and does not seem to know what to do. She tries to explain why the teacher did it. The teacher tries to invite Tom to go and listen to the story, but he does not go. He picks up some toys from a cupboard and starts throwing them on the floor. His desperate crying changes to furious shouting. Mother says this happens every day.

In this painful scenario, we see how Tom tries to cope. His attempts to obliterate his anxiety are unsuccessful. He tries to inflict his distress about the potential loss of someone he wants to cling to onto someone else by grabbing the other child's car just after he sees his mother about to leave. This is an attempt to modify his pain by projecting it onto someone else, and is a typical defence that is used in the presence of persecutory anxiety. The other child is to have something taken from him and suffer.

Through the interventions of the teacher, when the car is handed back to the child, Tom is forced to have the pain he cannot yet bear. His mother does not know how to contain him in this state, and all he can do is try to evacuate distress by throwing himself and all the toys on the floor, which is another attempt at evasion and a typical response to a communication-rejecting container. He cannot think; he just acts.

Through the intervention of the observer, Paulo, who spent time each day observing the child, Tom seemed to learn a different method of coping with pain over time, perhaps through identifying with the thoughtful approach of the observer.

In contrast, three weeks later Tom is sitting on the floor with many toys. He has a piece of cloth in his mouth and is sucking it. [*Was this how he tried to keep hold of his infant self's connection to his mother?*]

He holds a pistol in his right hand and a little

plastic elephant in his left. With the fingers of his right hand, he touches the elephant's eyes and at the same time drops his pistol to the ground. [*Was Tom focusing on the eyes and seeing, perhaps realising, rather than needing to hold on to the methods of the obliterating gun?*]

He takes a little and big elephant and clears a space in front of him; he then makes the small elephant feed from the big one. He has to grasp the two animals all the time, or they would fall. He tries leaving them several times and when they do fall, Tom looks at his mother and brings them back to their original positions. He seems curious about how they fell. [*Was this curiosity an identification again with the observer's curiosity? I remind you how Tom himself was falling in the first observations.*]

After a time, Tom's mother comes to him and asks what game he is playing. 'It is a game about animals who fall,' he says.

Mother smiles at him and says she has to go. He looks at her with desperate, tearful eyes and asks if she could stay with him one moment more.

Mother says she can't. She kisses him and walks out. Tom looks at his mother while she walks out, then bursts into tears. After a few seconds he stops crying. He dries his tears with his hands, stands up and comes near the observer, asking him to pick him up and 'take me to the window to see my mummy who is not there'.

The observer takes him in his arms and walks to the window. Tom stares out into the garden and after a few minutes of silent gazing asks to be put down and runs off to play with the other children.

Tom was trying to symbolise his experience, which served the function of naming and binding the anxiety. He seemed to be thinking in the sense of creating a space, trying to make sense of his emotional experience where a mother and baby can be together, but who separate (fall), and then come back together (are stood up). It has all the hallmarks of a container mother and a contained baby.

If Tom can internalise and hold on to this representation, which allows him to realise the facts of the situation he is in, his anxiety seems to be modulated. He copes with the pain in a different way. He does not inflict it on someone else but carries it himself, perhaps with the help of this internal object like the big elephant, who can help him, as the baby, contain it and bear it. This is more of a depressive reaction to his situation. His ability to 'see a mummy who is not there' suggests that he has an internalised representation of a mother and baby in his mind, who can be together and apart, and then come back together again. His silent gazing while being contained by the arms of the observer may have been how he looked into his internal space to find this internal mother and baby representation.

The ability to tolerate the frustration of the presence of a 'not there mummy' long enough to create a thought about it, which Tom verbalised, is a crucial developmental step. His thinking modulates his anxiety and also gives rise to hope.

The presence, then, of an internalised object (in the form of a functioning container/contained system) to receive distress and think about it (based on identification with these functions having been performed externally for the child) is crucial in developing his capacity to deal with all mental pain in a growth-enhancing manner – that is, to bear it in a manner that leads to thought. We are now in a position to return to the anxieties involved in learning and growing up, or in dealing with any new situation.

Knowing and Not Knowing: Anxieties Involving Learning, Growth and Development

For many children, growing up is not conceived of as learning to take responsibility for one's self. For many young children, it is felt as a way to shed one identity and assume a new one . 'I'm a big boy/girl now.'

This usually means finding someone else to have the baby feelings or little feelings, as growth is not conceived as organic and developmental, starting from the roots in the infantile ground and growing up from there.

True learning and growing is a painful experience and involves a lot of anxiety. For learning to take place, a certain amount of frustration is inevitable – the frustration of not knowing something, or of being confused and anxious about being ignorant. The capacity to bear these feelings determines the capacity to learn. This pain is essentially the 'uncertainty cloud'[30] or the ability to tolerate uncertainty, 'without irritable reaching after fact and reason', defined as *negative capability* by Keats.[31] This refers to the ability to tolerate the uncertainty of a new idea/situation impacting on the old ideas and ways of functioning that necessitates change. All 'facts of the external world are knowable only by their secondary qualities as they impinge on our senses in the context of an emotional experience. The ability to think about these facts of an emotional experience requires that the emotionality, especially the [anxiety], is contained'.[32]

The difficulty of bearing the anxiety of feeling little is illustrated by the following example of four year old Alison. Alison was immaculately dressed by her mother as a little adult. She carried herself with an air of superiority and haughtiness. She seemed above it all. Her mother used to drop her off at the nursery and stalk off, not saying goodbye, but leaving Alison unmoved; she was a big girl, big girls don't cry, only babies cry.

On one occasion, Alison sees her friend Molly by the climbing frame with another girl, Victoria. She walks over to them, hovering nearby. No one greets her. Molly then turns to Alison and says, 'I've got navy sandals.'

Alison replies scathingly, 'No, don't be silly; they're navy blue.' [*We call this a put down, because it is putting another down, in an attempt to raise yourself up.*]

Molly and Victoria go inside. Alison follows a few steps behind. The girls move over to the book corner and sit looking at some books. Molly enthusiastically comments on the pictures in her book. Alison, on the other hand, sits cursorily flicking through the pages of a book, not seeming to take things in, but appearing to be reading. Molly makes fun of an *Aladdin* book, saying that 'Aladdin is a girl'. Alison rather sharply retorts, without looking up from her book, 'It's not an *Aladdin* book; it's not that front, it's the other front.'

Molly is confused.

Here we see Alison as a know-it-all, putting up a front, who makes others confused. She wants to give an impression of a big girl who doesn't care by projecting herself into a big grown-up identity as someone who knows how to read and corrects the silly little children. The caricatured quality of the pseudo little adult is evident, as littleness and confusion is projected elsewhere.[33]

In Melanie Klein's original formulation, depressive anxiety was thought to be developmentally more advanced than persecutory anxiety. Bion, however, was able to show that all of us oscillate between the two sets of anxieties.

It is common for the pain, especially guilt, inherent in depressive anxiety to be too intense to be contained and managed, and usher the return of more persecutory feelings. Premature feelings of guilt experienced by a person not capable of bearing them can feel extremely persecuting. Similarly, persecutory feelings may give rise to depressive feelings.

A simple illustration of the latter situation was afforded when a ten year old boy crept downstairs on the morning of his birthday and opened all his presents before other members of the family woke up. He knew that this was not what usually happened on birthdays. When his parents woke up they were appalled; they felt angry and cheated.

At first the boy was uncaring, but then became terribly upset when he saw how spoilt things had become. He knew he had wrecked his birthday morning, having looked forward to it for so long. He cried bitterly and painfully, saying, 'Why did I do it? I didn't think. Please, please forgive me.'

He was able to use the experience and see that half the pleasure of getting presents is the sharing with others of the experience of giving and receiving. Having deprived others of this, he had deprived himself as well.

The child's couldn't-care-less, self-centred attitude had given way to depressive anxiety, which was very painful when he saw the damage he had done. With the help of his parents he was able to manage it and learn from experience.

Nameless Dread, Naming and Failures of Containment

Bion describes a situation in which the infant, fearing that he is dying – that is, suffering from the primary anxiety about dissolution as described earlier (see pages 11–12) – projects this anxiety into his mother, or container.

A well-balanced mother can accept [this anxiety] *and respond therapeutically – that is, in a manner that makes the infant feel it is receiving its frightened personality back again, but in a form that it can tolerate – the fears are made manageable for the infant personality.*[34]

If, however, the mother cannot accept these projections into her and perform the function of containment for the infant, he may take back into him an experience of his feeling having been stripped of meaning, and thus receive back what Bion has called 'nameless dread'. This is worse than the fear of dying itself, since it is unbound by a name and thus manifests itself as a feeling of dread that cannot be located.

This scenario is common in people who have serious illnesses and cannot let themselves know that the feeling they have is a fear of dying. Instead, they carry within them a worse feeling of nameless dread. Very often, those people around the very ill person are also so overwhelmed by anxiety themselves at the potential loss of their loved one that they cannot think clearly and help the ill person name and contain his/her experience. People often try to 'protect' the ill person, by using euphemisms or false reassurance, rather than helping the ill person and themselves face the facts of their lives.

To name an experience of anxiety binds it. A name is used to prevent the scattering of phenomena, because it describes the elements of an experience as being interrelated. As Bion says:

Having found the name and thereby bound the

phenomena, the remainder of history, if so wished, can be devoted to determining what it means. The name is an invention to make it possible to think about something before it is known what that something is.[35]

It is extremely persecuting to live in an unnamed universe. It leads to what is termed 'free floating anxiety' which cannot be located. Anxiety can feel everywhere.

Susan, aged ten, told her therapist that she could not sleep at night. She thought something was under her bed. It might be a cat, she thought; but the cat was on the other side of the room. Then she said it might be zombies with their arms stretched out in front of them; these zombies wanted the blood of humans by biting their necks. But then Susan worried that her house had a ghost in it because the TV channels spontaneously changed. The ghost, called James, was a friend of her mother's who had died of a heart attack. They also had sharks in their fishtank at home, and rats were a problem, too. At this point, Susan pulled up the hood of her jumper. Then she put her finger into her mouth and bit it really hard.

Susan is a little girl whose anxiety is located all over the place and seems to shift about with alarming rapidity. It does not come to rest anywhere, but floods her. Her hard biting on her finger may be her way of giving the pain a definite location, as discussed in the case of the self-harming adolescent (see page 21).

Failures of containment give rise to all kinds of anxiety. Panic attacks occur when there is no containment of anxiety and the person feels flooded with unprocessed, unnamed emotion that is often discharged into somatic disturbances. The fear and anxiety engendered by the thought of a panic attack is enough to trigger such an attack.

The failure of an attachment figure to contain anxiety can also mean that instead of the anxiety being 'named' and bound, it is returned to the person in an intensified form, as in the nameless dread situation. The person then has to deal with a double dose of anxiety, since he has the original anxiety projected back into him in an intensified form, together with the anxiety that no container exists for him – and so he feels misunderstood.

I observed an example of this in an aeroplane which hit a patch of turbulence. A child looked up at its mother's face to read from her, 'What am I supposed to feel about this situation?'; this was clearly anxiety-provoking, as the plane shuddered and bumped. The mother's face was ashen, conveying the emotions of someone in a supposed life-threatening situation. The child instantly became hysterical, as he was not only having to cope with his own anxiety unaided, but also seemed to receive a full blast of his mother's anxiety which then completely overwhelmed him.

Premonition of Emotion

If we return to Bion's definition of anxiety, as 'premonition of emotion', and accept that emotions are at the heart of our human existence, then anxiety, too, and how we deal with it, also occupies a central place.

Damasio, a neuroscientist, convincingly argues that emotion assists reasoning and that neurological evidence suggests that 'well-targeted and well-deployed emotion seems to be a support system without which the edifice of reason cannot operate properly'.[36] This is congruent with Bion's ideas that thinking arises out of containment of emotional experiences.

The ability to regulate emotional states is thus crucial for social, emotional, cognitive and neurobiological development.[37] This can only happen if the infant has the experience of an intimate relationship to an attachment figure who is emotionally attuned to him. If there are chronic disturbances in this for any reason, the baby never learns how to contain his own emotional states and cannot cope with the intensity of intimate relationships. The child's capacity to cope with anxiety thus predicates how well he will cope with life itself.

Notes

1. Hinshelwood, R. D., *A Dictionary of Kleinian Thought*, London: Free Association Books, 1991, p. 218.

2. Rycroft, C., *A Critical Dictionary of Psychoanalysis*, Harmondsworth: Penguin, 1968, p. 8.

3. Bion, W. R., *Elements of Psychoanalysis*, London: Heinemann, 1963, chapter 16, pp. 74–7.

4. Hinshelwood, op. cit., p. 221.

5. Laplanche, J. and Pontalis, J. B., *The Language of Psychoanalysis*, London: Hogarth Press and Institute of Psychoanalysis, 1985, p. 48.

6. Freud, S., 'Inhibitions, Symptoms and Anxiety', *Standard Edition of the Complete Psychological Works of Sigmund Freud*, vol. 20, London: Hogarth Press and Institute of Psychoanalysis, 1926, p. 77–175.

7. Hinshelwood, op. cit., p. 221.

8. Rycroft, op. cit., p. 8.

9. Freud, op. cit., pp. 77–175.

10. Rycroft, op. cit., p. 8.

11. Laplanche and Pontalis, op. cit., pp. 189–90.

12. Bowlby, J., *Attachment and Loss*, vol. 1 (*Attachment*), London: Hogarth Press, 1969/1982.

13. Hopkins, J., 'The observed infant of attachment

theory', *British Journal of Psychotherapy*, no. 6, 1990, pp. 460–71.

14. Ward, I., *Introducing Psychoanalysis*, Cambridge: Icon Books, 2000.

15. Perry, B. D., Pollard, R. A., Blakley, T. L., Baker, W. L. and Vigilante, D., 'Childhood trauma, the neurobiology of adaptation, and "use dependent" development of the brain: how states become traits', *Infant Mental Health Journal*, 16, 1995, pp. 271–91.

16. Klein, M., 'On the theory of anxiety and guilt', *Envy and Gratitude and other works. Writings of Melanie Klein*, vol. 3 (1948), London: Hogarth Press and Institute of Psychoanalysis, 1975, pp. 25–43.

17. Joseph, B., 'Envy in everyday life', in *Psychic Equilibrium and Psychic Change. New Library of Psychoanalysis* (chapter 13), *Selected Papers of Betty Joseph*, Bott Spillius, E. and Feldman, M. (eds), London: Tavistock/Routledge, 1989, p. 186.

18. Klein, M., 'A contribution to the Theory of Intellectual Inhibition', *Love, Guilt and Reparation and other works. Writings of Melanie Klein*, vol. 2 (1931), London: Hogarth Press and Institute of Psychoanalysis, 1975, pp. 236–47.

19. Hinshelwood, op. cit., p. 112.

20. Meltzer, D., 'Terror, Persecution and Dread', *Sexual States of Mind* (chapter 14), Perthshire: Roland Harris Trust Clunie Press, 1979, p. 105.

21. Meltzer, op. cit., p. 105.

22. Bion, W. R., *Learning from Experience*, London: Heinemann, 1962, p. 73.

23. Joseph, B., 'Different types of anxiety and their handling in the analytic situation', in *Psychic Equilibrium and Psychic Change. New Library of Psychoanalysis* (chapter 7), *Selected Papers of Betty Joseph*, Bott Spillius, E. and Feldman, M. (eds), London: Tavistock/Routledge, 1989, p. 108.

24. Klein, M., 'A contribution to the Theory of Intellectual Inhibition', *Love, Guilt and Reparation and other works. Writings of Melanie Klein*, vol. 1 (1931), London: Hogarth Press and Institute of Psychoanalysis, 1975, pp. 240–1.

25. Hoberman, M. A., *A House is a House for Me*, Harmondsworth: Penguin, 1986.

26. Beaumont, M., 'The effect of loss on learning', *Journal of Educational Therapy*, vol. 2, 1991, pp. 33–47.

27. Bion, W. R., *Learning from Experience*, London: Heinemann, 1962.

28. Meltzer, D. and Harris, M., 'A Psychoanalytical model of the child-in-the-family-in-the-community' (1976), in *Sincerity and Other Works. Collected Papers of Donald Meltzer*, Hahn, A. (ed.), London: Karnac Books, 1994, p. 387.

29. Carignani, P., 'An observation in school with a 22 month old child', Paper given at the opening of the Centro Studi Martha Harris, Palermo, Sicily, 1994.

30. Bion, W. R., *Elements of Psychoanalysis*, London: Heinemann, 1963, p. 42.

31. Quoted in Bion, W. R., 'Letter to George and Thomas Keats, 21 December 1817', *Attention and Interpretation* (chapter 13), London: Heinemann, 1970, p.125.

32. Meltzer, D. and Harris, M., op. cit., p. 412.

33. Emanuel, R., 'The child-in-the-family-in-the-nursery', *The Psychology of Nursery Education*, London: Freud Museum/Karnac Books, 1998, pp. 43–65.

34. Bion, W. R., 'A Theory of Thinking', in *Second Thoughts. Selected Papers on Psycho-Analysis* (chapter 9), New York: Jason Aaronson, 1962, pp. 114–15.

35. Quoted in Bion, W. R., 'Letter to George and Thomas Keats, 21 December 1817', *Attention and Interpretation* (chapter 13), London: Heinemann, 1970, p. 87.

36. Damasio, A., *The Feeling of What Happens. Body, Emotion and the Making of Consciousness*, London: Heinemann, 1999, p. 42.

37. Schore, A., 'Attachment and the Regulation of the Right Brain', in (eds) Steele, H. and Cassidy, J., *Attachment and Human Development*, London: Routledge, 1999.

Bibliography

M. Beaumont, 'The effect of loss on learning', *Journal of Educational Therapy*, vol. 2, 1991.

W. R. Bion, *Learning from Experience*, London: Heinemann, 1962.

W. R. Bion, 'A Theory of Thinking', in *Second Thoughts. Selected Papers on Psycho-Analysis* (chapter 9), New York: Jason Aaronson, 1962.

W. R. Bion, *Elements of Psychoanalysis*, London: Heinemann, 1963.

W. R. Bion, 'Letter to George and Thomas Keats, 21 December 1817', in *Attention and Interpretation*, London: Heinemann, 1970.

J. Bowlby, *Attachment and Loss*, vol. 1 (*Attachment*), London: Hogarth, 1969/1982.

P. Carignani, 'An observation in school with a 22 month old child', Paper given at the opening of the Centro Studi Martha Harris, Palermo, Sicily, 1994.

A. Damasio, *The Feeling of What Happens. Body, Emotion and the Making of Consciousness*, London: Heinemann, 1999.

R. Emanuel, 'The child-in-the-family-in-the-nursery', *The Psychology of Nursery Education*, London: Freud Museum/Karnac Books, 1998.

S. Freud, 'Inhibitions, Symptoms and Anxiety', *Standard*

Edition of the Complete Psychological Works of Sigmund Freud, vol. 20, London: Hogarth Press and Institute of Psychoanalysis, 1926.

R. D. Hinshelwood, *A Dictionary of Kleinian Thought*, London: Free Association Books, 1991.

M. A. Hoberman, *A House is a House for Me*, Harmondsworth: Penguin, 1986.

J. Hopkins, 'The observed infant of attachment theory', *British Journal of Psychotherapy*, no. 6, 1990.

B. Joseph, 'Envy in everyday life', in *Psychic Equilibrium and Psychic Change. New Library of Psychoanalysis*, London: Tavistock /Routledge, 1989.

B. Joseph, 'Different types of anxiety and their handling in the analytic situation', in *Psychic Equilibrium and Psychic Change. New Library of Psychoanalysis*, London: Tavistock /Routledge, 1989.

M. Klein, 'A contribution to the Theory of Intellectual Inhibition', *Love, Guilt and Reparation and other works. Writings of Melanie Klein*, vol. 1 (1931), London: Hogarth Press and Institute of Psycho-analysis, 1975.

M. Klein, 'On the theory of anxiety and guilt', *Envy and Gratitude and other works. Writings of Melanie Klein*, vol. 3 (1948), London: Hogarth Press and Institute of Psychoanalysis, 1975.

J. Laplanche and J. B. Pontalis, *The Language of Psychoanalysis*, London: Hogarth Press and Institute of Psychoanalysis, 1985.

D. Meltzer, 'Terror, Persecution and Dread', in *Sexual States of Mind*, Perthshire: Roland Harris Trust Clunie Press, 1979.

D. Meltzer and M. Harris, 'A Psychoanalytical model of the child-in-the-family-in-the-community' (1976), in *Sincerity and Other Works. Collected papers of Donald Meltzer*, Hahn, A. (ed.), London: Karnac Books, 1994.

B. D. Perry, R. A. Pollard, T. L. Blakley, W. L. Baker and D. Vigilante, 'Childhood trauma, the neurobiology of adaptation, and "use dependent" development of the brain: how states become traits', *Infant Mental Health Journal*, 16, 1995.

C. Rycroft, *A Critical Dictionary of Psychoanalysis*, Harmondsworth: Penguin, 1968.

A. Schore, 'Attachment and the Regulation of the Right Brain', in H. Steele and J. Cassidy (eds), *Attachment and Human Development*, London: Routledge, 1999.

I. Ward, *Introducing Psychoanalysis*, Cambridge: Icon Books, 2000.

Acknowledgements

I would like to thank Adie, Alex and Louise Emanuel, Anne Hurley and Ivan Ward for their help in producing this book.